SOPHOMORE

SOPHOMORE STOMP

LISA DEVON

Chatter House Press
Indianapolis, Indiana

Sophomore Stomp

For information:
Chatter House Press
7915 S Emerson Ave, Ste B303
Indianapolis, IN 46237
chatterhousepress.com

ISBN: 978-1-937793-52-4

Dedication

This collection of poems is dedicated to my family, friends and fans. Your support reminds me that this work is larger than myself. Your love shows me the light of truth on days when I have trouble finding it.

Disclaimer
While reading these poems, nothing should be inferred about anyone living or dead. Not all of these stories are my personal truths. Assume artistic license has been liberally applied.

Table of Contents

Don't Tread on Me Either

Kum ba ya and such

Feminist Protection Products

Smile

The veil of congeniality grows thin
During this period
When the blood flows outside my veins
The burden of my second-class citizenship
Grows along with my task list
And becomes too heavy for me to bear alone
The pain in my belly has been handed down to me
From centuries of my sisters being treated like property

Your gaze has turned my womb
into a breeding ground for your judgement
I can only get ahead, if I'm willing to give head
And be patted on the head and the behind

Success demands that I am smarter than everyone else
But not so much that I am a threat
While also being pleasant and pretty
The fine lines you force me to walk
Have become blurred,
But of course,
That's my fault
For forgetting that above all
I am a decoration

Everything I wear is an invitation for your criticism
You're still trying to convince me
That your misogyny is my privilege
Cat calls in the street are a compliment
I should be flattered
Some girls never get that
They are too old or too fat
Beats invisibility
Cat called in the street
But ignored in the boardroom

Unless I'm pouring the coffee or taking lunch orders
Not ignored when he forces his body against mine in a deserted hallway
Pinning me against the wall
Assuring me no one has ever made him feel this way before
But I don't want to FEEL YOU ON MY PERSON

What about MY feelings?
My feelings about my mistreatment
Are blown off as "female excitability"
Having feelings at all damages my credibility
While I have to massage the delicate male ego
on the daily
Just to navigate life
in the narrow lane in which I'm allowed to exist
And when I stand up for myself
The tiniest push back is seen as an attack
The cause of my anger must be of my own doing
I must be bleeding

Because men can't accept that I might be upset
About their treatment of HALF the population

"Why don't you smile, pretty lady?"

Because I am hurrying to my second job
Which I need
Because none of the things I can do
Are valued
Trapped in society's glass menagerie
Where I am the featured creature
A beautifully displayed workhorse
I can't even escape this trap
Much less, rise to the top
Like women should
as we ARE the cream of the crop
So, we work twice as hard

For half the pay he gets
He has a family to support, you know
(like I don't)
I WOULD like to know
How can I be too fragile to open a door,
But tough enough to work full time
Inside AND outside the home?

While I work myself to death
I'll be sure to stay alluring and demure
Proving that I'm pure
And worthy of your respect
Demeaned, diminished in every aspect of society
I won't be judged on my piety
Imma hold my head high and be mighty
Even when you call me flighty
Because I have twice as much opportunity as my grandmother
And I plan to use it wisely
So my granddaughter will have twice as much as me
But only if we continue to demand our equality
With overwhelming solidarity
No one ever stopped being oppressed easily
The system is rigged to keep us down
So, you'd better fight
like you have an Uzi under your bullet-proof gown
FOR OUR EQUALITY

I don't know about you,
But I'm tired of being

Underestimated
Undervalued
Belittled
Ignored
Objectified
Passed over

Brushed against
Mitigated
Shamed
Victim-blamed
Disbelieved
Disenfranchised
Denied healthcare

Told to just smile and be nice
I'M JUST SICK OF IT

Even though in my lifetime
"We've come a long way, baby"
But we still got a long ways to go!
NEVER. STOP. DEMANDING.
EQUAL. TREATMENT.
When we get it,
Then, we smile.

Macho Man

I'm a macho man
Ready to get down
With any woman I can
Hey baby – how you doin'?
Yeah, I know you want some of this
I could get her

Cause I'm a man. I'm THE man
I open doors for women
Let them pass through first
So I can look at that ass in a skirt
Or hold it open so she has to
Brush against me through the doorway
So I can feel her electricity
And smell her hair
Remind her
That I'm a man
I do important things
I deserve more money because
I have to support a family
As soon as I find a wife
She has to be pretty
Not too fat
Unless she has big tits
And can cook
Cause my wife will cook for me
And clean my house
And take care of my children

Cause I'm a REAL MAN
After all, I have a gun
It's right here baby,
And I'm not afraid to use it
You want some of this

I work out
For real, I own a gun
And a sweet ride
She's my current bride
I spend all my money on her
But she never says "No"
Wives can't say "No", ya know?
She agreed to this
Or she will
Once I find her
And make her mine
Because if I love her
She HAS to marry me
And be my wife
I've seen it in the movies
And on TV
I will send her flowers
And wait outside her job
To take her to lunch
She won't need to work
Once we get married
I will take her out on dates
That she finally agreed to
After like, 100 texts
When I take her home
I'll kiss her
And push her against the front door
And keep kissing her
Until she realizes she loves me
I love women

Cause I'm a REAL MAN
Except women at work
They're the worst
The ones who don't know their place
They keep having all these ideas

And trying to talk in meetings
Worse than that
They keep asking if you did stuff
Who does that bitch think she is?
I won't be questioned
Doesn't she know
I'm A MAN
So I don't make mistakes
It's my secretary's fault
If something isn't done
She's just a dumb girl
Of course I'm worth 5 times her salary
I'm a man
I'm large and in charge
I take up space
Because the whole world
And everything in it belongs to me

So I can't stand it when these mean girls
Keep trying to show me up
And make me look like a fool
Like your master's degree and PMP
Make you smarter than me?
I'M A MAN
I don't know why we let women work here anyway
Everyone knows men are much smarter
I guess it does make for some nice scenery at work
But those bitches better stay outta my way
If she thinks she's going to get promoted over me
She's crazy
If that does happen
I'll just take her into the conference room
And show her
Who's the boss

She dresses like such a slut
You know she wants it
And I can give it to her
Because
I'M A MAN
LARGE AND IN CHARGE
I take up space
Because the whole world
And every woman in it
Belongs to me!!

FAT

When I was just a girl
I learned that the worst thing a girl could get --
Was FAT
In fact, I was put on my 1st diet at 6 months old
By the time I was 5 or 6
I had heard that story a dozen times
I was a tall child
Always the tallest in my class
Therefore, the largest
Not tall and skinny, of course
I was solid and beefy
I already knew that I was the biggest
And that wasn't good, not for a girl

What I didn't realize I was learning is that
Society owns the standard on beauty
And anyone is allowed to weigh-in on the size of yours

As I reached puberty
I was still one of the tallest kids
My hips grew to provide my womanly frame
With a solid foundation
Just as they were supposed to
Also growing was my mother's worry
As she admitted,
"I think you need the next size up,
Those are tight in the seat."
Her nose wrinkled when something didn't fit right
"That makes you look fat!"
She would announce
"Better get the next size up"
She was horrified

As a tiny woman, barely 5 feet tall
STILL, at almost 70, a size 6
I don't blame her.
I knew my size 13 body was an abomination

I had 2 female cousins, one a bit older, one a bit younger
Both impossibly skinny
The women in my family are small,
Even the tall ones are thin
Because the absolute WORST thing a woman can get
Is FAT
My senior year of High School
The older cousin got married
As a bridesmaid,
I had to get fitted for a dress
The woman who measured me said,
"Ooh, you have perfect measurements,
36, 26, 36, so we will order you the size 12"
I was both excited and confused by this statement
Because perfect and size 12 didn't seem to fit together

My father called me a "stallion"
Referring to my juicy hips and thighs
He already knew that men of color
Would appreciate my shape,
He warned me of their attention,
But I also heard the part he didn't say
Being more attractive to black men than white
Was somehow a failure, of mine.

My tall skinny sister
He called a "stalk"
Short for beanstalk
Not statuesque
Not model-esque
Not ever, just right

I thought Stallion was better than that
And I had plenty of male attention
So, I didn't worry too much
Except every time I tried on new clothes
Or had to dress up for something
OK, I worried about it a lot!

I thought I was the fattest of all my friends
I remember there was one cheerleader who was a curvy girl
She was so pretty and sweet
She gave me hope
That big girls can be pretty,
That maybe,
I
Could be pretty

My first year of college
I had too many things to do
So, I gave up sleeping
And got an ulcer
I lost my lunch every day
Until I stopped eating lunch
I was a size 9 and HOT
And I still don't really eat baloney

A few years later
I was happy, I think
But for some reason,
Probably birth control
I put on 15 lbs. in 2 months
EVERYONE commented on it.
I thought,
Well, all my life I've been told I was fat
Now I really am fat
It was my destiny

I moved to Indiana
Where I quickly put on 20
Protective, insulating pounds
But I still found a boyfriend
He has a "washer and dryer" stomach
So he never complains about my curves
And he plies me with cookies
So he must like at little extra meat on the bones

A few years later
While I was carrying that man's child
I was diagnosed with Gestational Diabetes
Now a doctor has confirmed that I am fat
Even while pregnant
I am somehow fatter than I should be
My diet, exercise, weight and blood sugar
Are closely monitored
Pregnancy is the only time a woman is "allowed"
To be fat
And I wasn't allowed
I was pissed.
As I ate healthy foods and exercised
I discovered that it makes me feel amazing
Now that I know the difference
I realize I have literally felt bad
Every single day of my life
Not because I thought I was fat,
The worst thing a woman can get is FAT
Because I was eating crap,
I felt like crap
Bad Food = Absolutely equals = Bad Mood
I still have depression
But a whole lot less
And I know how to fix it, mostly

So I maintained the diabetes diet and lifestyle
And the same weight 188 lbs.
After having 2 babies
For 15 years
I felt OK,
Still kinda fat
Wearing a size 12 or 14
I was glad it wasn't an 18
My mother DID teach me how to dress for my shape
For that I am eternally grateful
She also gave me
My constant judgement of "FAT" people (including me)
Which I could do without
But I did the best I could
With what I had
And I looked good

So almost a year ago
I discovered I am allergic to wheat or gluten
Which I have enjoyed my whole life
I was a 2-biscuit girl
Then a one biscuit woman
Now I am a woman who just wants biscuits

When I stopped eating wheat,
A miracle happened
25 pounds just fell off me
I was a slacker on the exercise
And I went back to eating French Fries
My hips and knees stopped aching
Even before the weight came off
I felt lighter and more energized
20 years younger
Although I had been eating 6 times a day for years,
The hungries, just went away

Now I am nearly 50 years old and I wear a size 8
For the first time in my life
This is the smallest I have ever been
Since puberty
I was a size 13 at 13

I had already acquired a degree of confidence that comes with age
Where you just can't be bothered
About what people think anymore
But being this slim takes me to a new level
Where you can't tell me nothing!!!
Where I can wear leggings as pants
Because I am a skinny bitch now,
I do what I want

The smaller I get,
The more I judge FAT people
Because I used to be one
I might have done one thing right
In my lifetime of thinking, I'm not OK
I'm not good enough because I am too fat
I can take that off my list of failures
Because girls are taught to strive for perfection
In looks and actions
And punished when they miss the mark
Where boys are rewarded for little to no effort
And never held accountable for their behavior
Turning it back on us and our appearance
Once again,
That is the only thing that matters as a woman
Because we all know
The worst thing a woman can get
Is FAT.

Drumstick

Smoldering
Smoky flavor
Wafting towards me
Blackened skin holds all
Juices in, savory smell
Watering my mouth
Teasing my belly
In anticipation
Of the first bite
Of that tender
Tasty flesh
Perfectly
Grilled
A dinner
That
Fits in
My hand.
Best damn
Drumstick
In all the
land

Dear Gluten,

I miss you already and I can't even leave you. You are bad for me, of course I love you.

I love biting through the crispy outside of a biscuit into the soft, warm, doughy center. Then savoring the taste as the goodness dissolves. Mmmmmmm

Same for sweet, corn hush puppies. Cheddar bay biscuits; freshly baked, crusty French bread with herbed butter.

I love a whole grain waffle with peanut butter and cinnamon.

I love a greasy, crispy, grilled cheese sandwich.

I love brownies, fresh out of the oven, mushy, chocolatey, delight

Homemade chocolate chip cookies call my name, luring me to the kitchen with their intoxicating aroma. Melting in my mouth. The Tollhouse tastes so good, there should be a toll on this house.

Just baked gluten is hard to resist, especially for the baked. Toasty edible pieces of love cooked just for me. And I love you so much. I wished you loved me too.

But Gluten you find your way to all my weaknesses. Fill in my joints with your aches. Leaving every cell in my body inflamed. Soreness and pain fatigue me. The bread chums the water, awakening the savage beast that is my hunger. Allergy symptoms overcome me, dragging me down, into a river of snot, taking my resolve and will power with it.

So please know that I love you more than life itself. It pains me so much to say "No" to you. But it pains me even more to say, "Yes". When I can remember that, I will feel much better. But you tempt me, you tease me, you taunt with the smells of home, reminding me of your delicious taste.

To add to my pain, I have to be THAT Basic Bitch,
Going "Is that Gluten-free?"
Maybe I would rather you think I'm basic, so you don't find out I am only

a diploma and a dental plan away from being white trash.
That's why I wear this Becky disguise, so clearly, I can't be seen with any
White Bread. So, I'm sorry Gluten, but it's over between us.

I will not miss the way you hugged me tight around the middle.
Embracing me with your pillowy softness, creating more of me to love.
But it melts further away, every day I avoid you.
Because I know I will see you around. You will ALWAYS be around.
Please understand I AM IGNORING YOU.
So, don't try to catch my eye with your pretty designs, and surround me
with your scent straining my stamina. My mouth wants you so badly,
while the rest of my body silently screams, "NO"!
I am having some fruit instead, please leave me alone.

And don't you DARE try to set me up with your ghastly cousin "Gluten-
free." He is you in the way that Tootsie Rolls are chocolate.

I won't have it.
I can't have it.
I love you, Gluten
Good bye!

Love,
Lisa

Good Feminist

Sometimes I forget to be a good feminist
After a lifetime of the world
Telling me
My only value is in my beauty
Sometimes I want to revel in it
My beauty, that is
I want to prance around in fancy
Matching bra and panties
Feeling like the hottest thing around
Like I finally did it
I got, I achieved it.
I nailed it.
I am beautiful, and therefore worthy
Then I remember that this pedestal of pretty
That I clambered my way onto
Is a trap
Keeping me hovering in a cloud of other people's opinions
Where I can't hit the ground running
Toward that things that I am supposed to do
And be and create
I forget that, when I take the bait
Wanting to be everything my TV tells me to be
I want to look like an underwear model angel
So I can share my secret garden
With my husband
He deserves that
I deserve to be that

But I wish I didn't want to be that
I wish it were OK to not shave my legs
I want to think it's beautiful
But I don't
I think it's lazy
And itchy

And it's only OK in the winter
Why can't it be ok?
Why can't we be beautiful that way?
I am glad he never complains
Maybe he just looks away
I mean
He's still getting laid

Every time I want to be more,
Lookism leers its way in
And locks me up again
I want to be objective
But I keep getting objectified

I want to feel beautiful,
No matter how I look
NO, I want to feel worthy
When I KNOW
I'm not beautiful
I want to feel so OK
That I don't care
What other people think of me

I want to live in a world
Where I am valued
Because of how smart,
Creative and funny I am
No matter what I look like
Where I don't have to carry the burden
Of trying to be beautiful
And never feeling good enough

Then I remember
I am a feminist
I believe women are equal to men
And no one else defines me

Even when I know they're judging me
Just not giving a damn about it
Is what being a feminist means to me.

I will never stop promoting equality for all
Confident in my mind and heart
That make me worthy
No matter what anyone else thinks
About the way I look.

Me too

He's a masher
He's a flasher
He's a basher
Act differently,
But they all want to smash her

He's a boor, he's a letch, he's a creep
He's a louse
Don't ever go to his house
Or you'll be caught like a mouse
He will toy with you
Then ruin you
Telling everyone things that are untrue
Or you wish
were untrue

He's a scoundrel, a cad and a rake
Seeing his creepy face makes me quake
But I have to make nice with Lothario
Who fancies himself the hero
In the story where he always gets the girl
He thinks he is some charming stud,
A smooth-operating, ladies' man
Chasing skirts like only he can
And I have to smile when I refuse his advances
Like on a different day he would have better chances
So he takes them, all

And I have to take it, all
because whomever can stomach his romances
is the one who advances
he's the only one allowed to give chances
Go along to get along
I am so fucking sick of that song

Perverts have now been exposed to the men
We women, always knew about them
That's why there are dozens of words of warning
For men like him
From the hundreds of women who have to put up with him

I know that you think you are a hunk
But believe me NO ONE wants to see your junk
If you can act right,
You might get lucky tonight
Meaning I won't call the police
About your debauchery
Trying to inflict your fantasies on me
Get your sleazy self away from me
Before I go to HR
Where no one will believe me
Or they do, but they won't sanction you
Because your animal urges are more important
Than my safety
And I should learn to protect myself

From mashers, flashers, bashers and smashers
From boorish louses
In creepy houses
From scoundrels, cads and rakes
Rejecting them with a smile on my face
Since I have to say it nicely,
When I say "NO"
He doesn't hear me
Right now, his feelings ARE more important than mine
Because there is always a chance
That my rejection
Will make him angry enough to kill me
That is a woman's reality
I just want to live my life
Safely

Am I still a Woman?

What makes a woman?
Is it the dresses?
The long tresses?

The beautiful breasts?
Is it my interests?

What if I love fishing?
And building things?
And destroying things?
And sports?

Am I still a woman?

What if I love other women?
Am I still a woman?

What makes me a woman?
Is it my ability to bear children?
What if I never do?
Am I still a woman?

What if my body can't?
Am I still a woman?

What if my hair is short?
And I can't stand dresses?

What if I have opinions?
And speak out?
And never cook?

What if I never do any of the "female" things
And do all of the "male" things?
Am I still a woman?
Why?

Just because I say I am?
Because Biology says I am?

Is it the level of pain
Discrimination and belittling
I am able to endure?
Is that what makes me a woman?

Is it in my looks?
What if I don't have the right curves?
Or if I have the wrong ones?

Am I still a woman?

Am I a woman because society says I am?
Or because I say I am?

I really need to know
Because my husband does a lot
Of "female" things
And I need to know if he is still a man
And I
Am still a woman

Because when we are entangled in this love together
It no longer seems to matter where he begins
And I end
Together we are a circle
With no end
No boundaries
To bind us

Hidden in plain sight
Where no one
Can find us

I become aware
That the distinctions between us
Are arbitrary

When dividing ourselves
Is impossible

We tethered together forever
Where we are all men
And we are all women

Because I am a person
And so are you

About that Mom life

Horriblize

(cw: cutting)

I learned a new word this week
Horriblize – v. to imagine horrible possibilities
In the absence of information
The brain will tell you lies
About the worst outcome it can devise

It is the prerogative of Mothers worldwide
Tell your ride
You can't be late
Your mom will worry

Oh, there I go making it all about me
Unfortunately
That's all I can do
Since whatever is wrong with you
Will probably get blamed on me

And you won't tell me
What I can do or
Why you are so distraught
You lash out against yourself

So I'm left to horriblize
And theorize

Maybe...
Maybe
Maybe

She didn't feel fierce enough
So she cut tiger stripes
Into her flesh
Scoring her own skin

Over and over again
Hoping to get a win
Over the demon within

Excising the enemy
With every slice
Exercising the right to
Modify her own body
Into that of a warrior
Scarring and marring herself
Hashmarks keeping score
Of her victories over the hater
Inside her head

Every trickle of blood
A record of her burning fear
Of failure
Of success
Of living another day on this planet

Etching her emotions
On her epidermis
She leeches the bad blood
Between her mind and soul
So they can kiss and make up
And maybe then
she can feel whole

Now it's a signal to the other warriors
She has the markings of her tribe
And she has survived
My baby is still alive
I want her thrive

.

Reading is Fundamental

(in response to school-wide, simultaneous, sustained, silent reading time, including the teachers)

Dear school leaders,
I KNOW
You're trying to raise
recreational readers

Get those kids a habit
As an author, I appreciate it,
But my kid
Is already an addict
And you exacerbate it
You can't give a junkie a hit
First thing in the day
You've told her it's time to play
Now her head is in that book
The rest of the day

She's not a casual reader
She really thinks the books need her
To devour and digest them
Recommend and respect them
Revere and protect them

When she was a toddler
She would close your book, paper or magazine
And say "The End"
Then maneuver her little rear end
Right into your lap with her book
As if to say "FEED ME"

This child lives to read
Books are the air she breathes
A vocabulary of nutritional nuggets
On which she feeds

Every chapter is a shot in the arm
She needs to survive
She loves books so much,
She worships in the library
praying at the altar of the author
sampling every sacrament
Her imagination a testament
This child doesn't just live to read
She reads to live

Oh, how my baby cried and cried
When her *Divergent* Tris died
She had to keep it all inside
Until she couldn't
And then she lied
Because no secrets
Will my reader provide
Since Tris' trilogy was still on my
Assigned reading list
She knew
I had not yet read this
She would not let me
Ease her pain
Because to her
Spoilers are not a game

I shouldn't be surprised
Because she
Literally cut her teeth
On board books
Consuming her favorites
Over and over again
Demanding "WEED IT!"

Then she told ME the stories
In picture books
Chewed through chapter books
Like candy
Then she moved on to comic books
Where she learned SHE could be a hero
Then Nancy Drew a line through
The Baby-Sitters Club and the Clique
Devouring each series, right quick
Reading everything she could get her hands on
Until one day, she decided,
"I'll Fly Away, through the Fault in Our Stars
With Percy Jackson and the Olympians,
on our way to Paper Towns"

That's when I KNEW
She was an addict
She knows it too
She's tried hard to succeed
By not taking her book
So she can't read
During science
Striving for compliance

Maybe, just maybe
She can turn her obsession
Into her profession
She's not just a bookworm
She's more of a book boa constrictor
Extracting their life force
To fuel her imagination
So she can cook up fanfiction
In some dystopian future kitchen

Because to her,
Reading IS fundamental

Promise

You were born when all of our hopes for the future
Manifested in human form
We filled you with our love
Nurtured you with our dreams
Invested everything we had in you
Sacrificing our free time to dote on you
Leveraging our future for yours
When we held you,
Tiny as you were,
You held so much promise
And we promised to do our very best for you
We really, really
tried

But you were never like the other children
Always preferring the adulation of adults to
Interaction with the other kids
Boy were those adults impressed with you and your vocabulary
Your peers, not so much
But you had so much to learn from them
I know you tried so much to act like them
They sensed your difference
and kept you at a distance

We thought that you would mature socially
That you would learn to complete assignments
And turn them in
That you would be happy
And make friends
That you would grow up
And figure it out
After all, you had so much promise
We poured all of our hopes and dreams into you
You were brilliant

You could do anything, hardly even trying
Things came to you so easily
We dreamed of all the things you could become
But all you ever wanted, was to be liked
by other kids
You wanted to be the center of attention all the time
But we couldn't do that for you
As your parents we could only love you
Honestly sometimes it was hard to like you
We thought loving you would be enough
But somehow
It never was

We gave you everything we had
Mortgaged our future for you
Borrowing against our own time
To pour into you
Everything we had
Reading and reasoning
Timeouts and treats
We tried every idea
Every parenting strategy
Every punishment
Every motivation
Eventually
We indulged you when we shouldn't have
Because we were tired
From giving and trying and giving
Pouring into your bottomless vessel
That couldn't be filled
And it was never enough
We could never convince you that we loved you
Fully, unconditionally, totally

Because every chiding, every criticism, every corrective word
Cut you to the quick
You couldn't stand to be corrected
You couldn't understand
We were only trying to make you better
The best you could be, in fact

Then we did the unthinkable
We gave you a playmate
A friend of your very own
All you saw was someone taking your spotlight
Dulling your shine with her baby cuteness
Taking up the time of your Mommy and Daddy
And now you have to help us take care of her
Because you're a big girl
A big sister now
And she is supposed to be your first friend
But from the first day
You were convinced
That we loved her more

She was sweet and beautiful
Kind, loving and gentle
Eventually you loved her too,
When she wasn't stealing your parents
You loved having someone to dominate
Someone to worship you

We continued to believe in the promise
That you were so brilliant
that you could be anything you wanted
That you could paint or write
That you could detect and discover
That you could lead
A rock band or engineering team
Anything you can dream,

As long as you were willing to work for it
But you weren't
There was nothing you were willing to work for
We tried to encourage you, and help you
But you wouldn't even help yourself
And you certainly never helped us
Eventually, after everything stopped being easy for you
You only excelled at excuses

When you became willful and defiant
We made the choice to be better than our parents
And NOT beat you into submission
I didn't want to break your strong spirit
You will need that someday
Many days
Cause you are hard-headed like your mother

In retrospect, that might have been a bad decision
I sure want to lay a hand on your smart mouth, now
But I can't afford it

It doesn't matter anyway
No punishment ever dissuaded you
Much less taught you a lesson
You push every limit to the breaking point
Because in your world,
The rules are for "other" people

We tried to still believe in the promise
As your brilliance started to fade
Arrested by your actual arrest
Attacked by your awful attitude
Bombarded by your boredom
Bulldozed by your buzz
Chained by your cheating
Cloaked in your cruelty

Drowned in your drama
Drained by your defiance
Eclipsed by your empty empathy
Failed by your forgery
Gobbled up by your greed
Halted by your hot head
Hidden by your highness
Lousy with your laziness
Looted by your lying
Poisoned by your pilfering
Stalled by your stealing
Soiled with your sloppiness
Tainted by your tall tales
Tattered by your treachery
Weakened by your whining

As much as we love you
We will be GLAD
To see you
Get your comeuppance

I feel like the stock market of my life crashed
And I lost half of my investments
I feel like I bet the wrong horse
Played the wrong slot machine
Like I'm tryna bluff a losing hand
But Lucy has taken away the football
One too many times
This sap isn't falling for the BS anymore

All we have left is your fervent, angry promise
To move out the day you turn 18

We hope it comes true
For when the drama machine is finally silenced
Your first friend will finally get her family back

Hating you

Hating you depresses me
I'm trapped in your toxicity
A noxious cloud, choking me

But loving you is worse
Your bottomless pit consumes me
There is so little love left for anybody
Else in the family

I guess I'll just go back to hating myself
Since that's what I'm best at

I marvel at how you are never wrong
And I am never good enough
Because I am the one who was supposed
To teach you
Right from wrong

And you know the difference very well
But it makes no difference to you
You get high off getting away with it
And you always get away with it
No one saw you steal that money from Mom's purse
So, you lie and deny till your dying breath

If you are caught, you quickly pivot
To blame the nearest stooge

That's why you keep them around
Plus, you need the worship
To keep yourself inflated

But you've conflated
Love and obligation
Or maybe you haven't
Because you know I am obligated
To provide for you
You are horrible to me

Most days my obligation is stronger
Than my love for you
But I hope my love can survive
Until you leave my home

I've seen flashes of it lately
It must really scare you
Since you react so harshly
Every time I am kind to you
You punish me

WHY must you be so contrary?
You're only agreeable when you want something

I just want out
I want to break up with you
Pack a bag and leave you
500 miles behind me
In my rear-view mirror
A cloud of dust envelopes you
And you disappear

And for a moment
I am free

Then the entire fetid contents of your room
Rains down on me
I am suffocating
And I will probably die

But I wake up in a padded room
Certain that I belong there
Cause I keep bouncing back and forth
Between trying to save you
And wishing you were--

I don't know how to help you
The only thing I haven't tried is illegal

Do I risk everything
For someone I can barely stand to be around?
It seems there is only one way to solve this
Because this is the part of the movie
Where the heroine has to be the bigger person
And save her enemy to prove her humanity
But it will take every ounce of her strength
To pull that demon back over the edge of the cliff
It is sure to lash out at her
While she saves it
And I save you,
Because I love you

Even with every awful thing
You've ever done to me,
I still love you
Because you are my baby
My first child
And hating you
Is killing me

Free Write

The would-be dictator
Of my domicile
Is in self-exile
Not gonna lie
It makes me smile
It's the most important mile
That separates us
So far, elevates us
Because I am elated
No longer weighted
Down
With your negativity
Wonder what you will do to me
Steal from me
Cheat me
Lie to me
Break my things
Shriek at me
But now
I'm free
I feel so light and airy
It's like I lost 180 pounds
Of bullshit
That was tied around my neck
I am free
I am free
I am free
Watch me soar
The day that I prayed for
Is here
My face hurts from smiling
Although I am afraid I'm going to
Jinx it

I really can't stop beaming
I feel like when I caught the
Holy Ghost for the first time
Revived, restored and renewed
Buoyed by the Grace of God
And I know the starting gates have been opened
The block on my blessings is gone
And now all the good things can get to me

I usually write poems about my misery
But in this one
The joy was about to burst out of me
It just had to go somewhere
I am a little frightened that it is not real
That it won't last
But I feel like the ghost
Of boyfriends past
Just stepped on the gas
And floored it right away from me
No more wheels spinning
Just taillights barely visible
And I am invincible
It's so unbelievable
And my face hurts from smiling
I have a runner's high
From crossing the finish line
Of this 18-year marathon
I am so excited
But I still might puke
Just to purge the rest of
The nonsense from me
I am free
I am free
I am free
I am ready to be me
Not just Mom

No longer a target
Of your misery
And feelings of inadequacy
I am free to just be me
Of course, I have another one to rear
But she's much less of a
Pain in the rear
I can finally hear
The call of the spirit in my ear
She says
You are free
You are free
You are a fully healed being of light
And you
Are
Free

Fix Your Face

He said he could fix my face
Fix it?
What is wrong with it?
Is it not decorative enough?
You want to fix it into a smile
A benign mask of approval
Fix my face?!
You'd betta not fix your face
To tell me that my face needs fixed
Cuz I'm fixed on facing my needs
Not on what my face needs
To be approved by you

My face is fixed
In neutrality
To best ignore you
And your invasive judgements
About what my face should look like
Because when I was young
I was told to fix my face
To wipe away any dismay
And to present
As quietly satisfied
But I wasn't
And I'm not
And I won't
Be told by some strange man
To fix my face

My face is fixed on my future
On a future where surgeons
And make-up artists don't
Fist-fight to see who can perfect me
Because "I"

Am already perfect
The Lord and I
Have fixed my face
To let my light shine through
And inspire you
By showing my truth
Not a desperate disguise of youth
Because I know my lined face
Has character and wisdom
You don't want me to embrace that

You want to be sure
I am not sure of myself
So I will stay chasing beauty
Instead of standing in it
Confidently

No one wants to admit that an older woman
Even exists
Or that she can be attractive
And valuable
And knowledgeable
And independent
And professional

Something happens between 35 and 65
Women just disappear
But more like erased
Or ignored
Right at the height of her power

Only to resurface
Resurfaced
Stretched and pulled
And plumped
Into a grotesque

Mask of youth
So she can be listened to
So she can preserve her
Desirability
To maintain visibility

So of course,
She has to fix her face
Because it's the only way
To save her space
In our youth obsessed world
Until she gives up
And emerges as a
Grandma or
Mimi or
Nana
Where she can be present again
Because she presents no threat
Her wisdom might even be respected
And no one expects her
To be desirable
Now she's the one
Telling people to fix their face

Work it, girl

Poems are starting to drip

Poems are starting to drip
From the hole that I'm biting in my lip
So the insults don't slip
Out
And wound you like a whip
Overturn your little ship,
Until you cease to even
Be a radar blip

But you can't stand me when I'm flip
Wounding ya with every quip
'Cause to best me, you're not equipped
Your vocabulary is an empty clip
And my style you will try to nip
But, if in my pool, you try to take a dip
You will drown in
Just
One
Sip
Of the nectar that flows from my lip
Where poems are starting to drip

And THAT'S when you started to trip
Careful you don't land on your tragically hip
Face it, kid
I'm a pip
And I belong on the Vegas strip
Until then,
I'm only here for a little kip
You know that check is a rip

So, take the chip
off
your shoulder
See if you could get ahold of
yourself
You better take THIS tip
and get a grip
On your attitude,
Or my lips
I will be forced to unzip!

Cube Farm

So, I signed on to this cube farm
I never expected to become a farmhand
But I am cultivating a farm, man
Plowing over the same ground
Hoping for a new outcome

Thin industrial carpet is the soil
Tilled by the turnover of new hires
Arranged in nice, neat rows of cubes
Each one filled with a human seed
Planted in its cozy nest
Watered -- by the cooler
Fertilized by the BS of endless meetings
Tiny new ideas poke through the nonsense
Ready to be nurtured
Ready to change the landscape
Straining to grow under fluorescent lights
Fueled up on the information superhighway
The little seedlings starting to take root
Smell like a bright future

But all I can smell is the salt
From the sea of acronyms, I'm drowning in
An alphabet assault of emails
Attacking interaction and communication
You see, my kind of flower
Withers in isolation

Tending my quiet office field
I pull away from the weeds of
Politics, lethargy, and indifference
That choke out my tender new shoots

while the steady hum of climate control
And the faint clicking of keyboards
Sound the indoor growth.
And the silence is deafening

Sacrificing my creativity
To water someone else's tree
Sometimes the futility overwhelms me
My eyes can no longer see
I turn my face toward the sky
So, every threatening tear
Falls back
Falls back
Falls back into its eye

This maddening exercise in redundancy
Will NOT get the best of me

Because farmhands must be vigilant
You see, fledgling innovations are often
Atrophied by apathy
The boxes blighted by boredom
The rot of dissention can spread quickly
Ruining an entire crop
The biggest threat to my farm is Darkness
Darkness
The lack of light
Coaxing the idea seedlings to life
Our sun is the World Wide Web
Often blocked by the failings of Internet Technology
Bringing out the darkness in humanity
No longer veiled in professional congeniality
Now, if you'll excuse me
I've got to get to a meeting
Because this compost is not going to turn itself

Face Lift

She needed a face lift

She'd grown old
And worn
Her vintage visage
Eroded by love
Her ready smile
Began to give way
Her once-smooth surface
Now pocked and pitted

It's time to be fitted
For a few upgrades
Her underside
Crumbling inside
Could use
Some shoring up
Reinforcing her
Bone structure
To stand up to
The future

Her strong shoulders
Sagging with exhaustion
Need a few supports
Dressed up like
A new pair of shorts
Covered with
Colored lines

I wish she could recover
In a far-off spa
So the ugly
Process wouldn't be on display
But for her
It doesn't work that way

She can never have an off day
She's survived two centuries
But she's got to be ready
For the next one

So lend her your sympathy
When you see under the bandages
All the way her to
Naked core
People working to restore
Her
To her former
Glory
Write the rest
Of her story

You should patiently endure
Unsightly scabs that ensure
A bright future
After all
Your underbelly isn't being retread

But it is difficult
Driving by her sick bed
Weaving through
On a tiny thread
The first building block
To the next level

Grateful
You are not being peeled
From your feet to your head
Then resurfaced and resealed
Restored and healed
To meet
Others needs
Like she is

Her suffering and sorrows
Are for your tomorrows

How dare you complain?
When we all feel her pain

Indianapolis
My sweet city
We all wish you
A speedy recovery
From your facelift

Buzz Words

The persistent use of buzz words
Is shaving my buzz – WORD!

Your musings on synergy
Are sapping my energy
Trying to get your bottom line padded
With something called "value added"

I can feel the glazing over of my eyes
While you strategize with strategic lies
So, you can optimize and maximize
Franchise and monetize

But you don't realize
Real gonna recognize
Real
That right there
Is otherwise
I have had my fill of your blustering blather
Creating a foamy lather
Of words
That don't matter

What are you trying to say?
Will have to talk in that corporate way?
Every day?
To be re-employed at my former pay?
That's not gonna play

Though I'm a weaver of words
And a teller of tales
When we get high off my vocabulary
We won't be using buzz words

Sandpaper

You say you "like me"
But only when I'm being
who you want me to be

You don't like the real me
The one who is coarse
And callous
And salty
Like my tears
No, you like
Who you would LIKE
Me to be
Who I could be
If I would just
Act like a lady
Internalizing a mountain of shoulds
For your comfort
But I refuse
And you regard me like refuse

Because you always
Rub me the wrong way
You are the sandpaper
Trying to soften my harsh edges
So that I am ground down
By the world

Polished into something
Smooth and shiny
You like me when I am pretty
But not when I'm petty
You like me when I am better
But not when I am bitter
You like me when I am out-spoken

But not when I've spoken out
For the longest time
I could never figure out
Why you irritate me so much
But now I know
It's your sandpaper judgement
Constantly wearing me away
Don't worry
I have an apology
Locked and loaded
Where I can be goaded
Into giving it to you
But it doesn't change the way I feel
Or the way I feel about you
So you can keep your ideas
Of what I should be
The
FUCK
Up
Off
Me

Fine Powder

The world has ground me into a fine powder
trying to erode my power
Wearing me away with its judgements
and expectations
But I can be reconstituted
Just add water
only a few drops
So that I become a thick, sticky paste
that clings to your synapses
Forcing you to think

My voice is loud and brash
making you hear truths
you'd rather ignore
Your answer to this is more
Just add more
water
until I become thinner and thinner
Spreading all around
but never really covering anything
Watered down
until I have become thin gruel
not enough to satisfy or nourish
Just a weak broth
without any bite
That's how I can be palatable
to the powers that be
that control stage entry

You want a watered-down version of me
because my power is frightening
You're afraid of my enlightening
the oppressed
having their needs addressed

Your double standards
make my ass
simultaneously too large
AND too small

My voice is shrill because
the truth hurts your ears
it will no longer be
whispered

I am here to dust
the talc of truth
all over you
Because the world has ground me
into a fine powder
concentrating me into
tiny crystals of power

Perfect

Some say the perfect
Is the enemy of the good
But perfect is the rival of good
Making it reach deep down inside
Pulling out the best that good has to offer

Striving for perfection
Always makes you better
Perfect is the carrot on the end of a stick
You can never reach
If you happen to reach perfection
You didn't get there by hard work alone
It also takes patience and will
And a few happy accidents
To reach the pinnacle of perfect

You'll find it a sharply pointed mountain top
Requiring all of your focus to balance there
When it begins to crumble underneath your feet
Landing you back
In mediocrity

Where you resume your journey
At an easy pace
But you can't help drifting
To the front of the pack
Where you belong
After all, you were once perfect
The memory of that drives you
Further, faster
Leaving good enough in the dust
Clawing your way to perfection
No matter who it hurts
Forgetting that it's an unstable

Table for one
But good, good has room for everyone
It takes some work to get there
And some will need assistance
But together we can all get there

When we remember that chasing perfection
Is that inspiration that will lead us to the
Common Good
As long as we recognize good enough
When we see it
And remember to be happy
Improving on good enough
Not haunted by perfection

Rabbit Hole of My Despair

OK Tightrope

It takes all my focus to stay on the OK tightrope
Any complaint or cross word is a step down
Into the rabbit hole of my despair
So, I concentrate on the good
On the positive

Shielding myself against the slights
Large and small that feel like an army
Attacking me
But it's really just me
Attacking myself
Preying on my own fears and insecurities

The slightest breeze
ruffles my feathers
I can turn it into an ill wind
in mere seconds
Poisoning myself with every thought
I am overwrought
Why am I trapped in this prison
Of my own making?

I know you think I'm faking
But you don't know
How my heart is aching
While I struggle to find balance
So I can stay on the OK tightrope

Where it's safe
Where everything is ok
Protected from distractions
and negative interactions

It takes all of my focus
To stay on the OK tightrope.
But I would like to upgrade
To a balance beam
Because my core has strength
But I need a larger
Margin for error
One with a bit less terror

Where the vessel
Suits the bearer
Of bad news
Who sings the blues
But likes to choose
Happiness

I wish happiness
Could be the net
Underneath the tightrope
But where's the drama in that?
When my old friend
ADHD robs me of my focus
I can always hold on to the
OK tightrope
Until my balance is restored

But it takes all my focus
To stay on the OK tightrope

Alphabet Soup

Endometriosis has left painful scars on my insides
My own body is fighting itself
I'm losing the internal, bloody battle
Month after month
But the worst pain of my disease
Comes from the tear it leaves

In my soul
My light begins to escape
Negativity seeps in
And starts to take over

I'm bouncing between
Anger and apathy
While anxious, annoyed and aggravated
I'm belligerent, cross and cranky
I'm defeated and defiant
Exhausted and frustrated
Gone are gregarious, happy and inquisitive
Instead I'm gassy, hormonal and impossible
I'm judgmental, killish, low-down and mean
Keenly aware of languishing in my own malice
I'm a noxious, ornery, pissed-off, railing super-bitch
Terrorized
by my own unkindness and vulnerability
I'm weary and exasperated
Yearning for Zen
Wondering
Why me?

Tear Factory

Sometimes
any harsh word
can make me cry
Every tiny frustration
and
every loving moment
like an AT & T commercial
any capturing of kindness
or example of love
Connects
with the Big Love inside of me
which grows too large to contain
and I am bawling
and I know
Today
is going to be weepy

I am a tear factory
where everyone is working overtime
with no breaks
and no brakes on the line
and no extra pay
dramatically increasing production
I am overwhelmed by the outpouring
of my feelings raining down on my face

Just thinking about that, makes me laugh
a little at first
Then the laughter inside gets so big
that it giggles
and giggles
and giggles
out of me
until I hyperventilate
and I can't breathe

This unscheduled break time
at the factory is over
As my eyes start leaking
building up to a full-on weeping
it's a good thing
I'm still laughing
although I have forgotten
what was so funny
I realize it must be me
Because I'm ridiculous
a sloppy mess of emotions
dialed up to 11

My feelings are magnified
distorting reality
until it's intensified
into another meltdown
I don't even know what started it
Maybe someone put a quarter
in the machine
that turns the rollercoaster
of emotions
that fuels the tear factory
inside of me

Double shifts leaving me spent
I can't put a name on my feelings
They are moving much too fast
to reach out and pick one
So, I gotta call out sick, hun
'cause the factory
is my responsibility now

I've heard the workers are going to strike
I hope it's soon
There is nothing

that I would like more
than to shutter that tear factory
Forever
Let it rust out and
become overgrown with ivy
so broken and barren
that not even
an evil genius
could get it started again

Thinking about that makes me smile so hard
that workers hear the alarms
I know they are cranking up again
as two hot tears escape
from the corners of my eyes
singeing my cheeks
producing liquid evidence
of the tear factory

Sack of Woe

(inspired by the 1960 Cannonball Adderley tune "Sack of Woe")

The weight of this sack of woe
Is so heavy, it grinds me into the ground
Curving my spine into an ache
Misery bubbles up from my belly
Grown in my womb, when nothing else is
My body betrays me –
As it is physically sad
Every time the potential for new life is washed away
The void is filled with the sorrow of a stillborn
Joy is drowned in a thousand thunderstorms

My brain is relieved not to be with child
But my body is devastated, again
My whole being was born for this
Each missed opportunity to grow life
Rips through me like
A kick in the gut that hurts all the way to my heart

My uterus literally mourns the life it could have grown
My heart is mad at me for living in this vessel alone
Like my body is a vehicle bringing souls from one plane to the next
At my age, I have run out of gas to fuel this train
Who is still giving out tickets?
This side-show of misery is about to overtake me

The cozy home for a new life lets go unwillingly
It goes kicking and screaming as it is released
It is insulted that its kind offer
to grow new life is rejected

At some point the pain
and punishment
will make you consider
trading in this torture
for a new kind
just give in to the desires
and demands of my body and
Grow a new person.

Ha ha ha
Not for me.
I won't worry the doctors
With a geriatric pregnancy

But yeah,
I need a sick day
Because my sack of woe
is spilling over
But I'll be ok
Tomorrow
See you then

Special Flower

Sometimes when I am skipping along through life
Making sure I enjoy the gift that is the present
Smelling the roses
I catch a whiff of the dark depression flower
Its alluring aroma is sweet at first
I am drawn in by its overwhelming power
I willingly rush into it
Looking for a comfortable place
That feels like home

And the flower envelopes me
In its pissed off petals
Fanning the flames of the anger
That lives inside me
The fire of my ire
Grows into a blaze
That is out of control
Burning everyone who comes near
Stay back,
I cannot protect you
It's all I can do to not
Burn everything down

The depression flower is flourishing
Inside me
It grows stronger
And I grow weaker
My rage swells until it pushes out
Everything else
Culminating in an ugly explosion
Saturating passersby

With the shrapnel from my soul
Leaving me spent
Lying among the leaves
Of the depression flower
Trying to become whole again

TKO

I know why they are called "bouts" of depression
I feel like I just went 12 rounds with my old nemesis
Depression snuck up on me
And sucker-punched me, right in the gut!

I absorb blow after blow
Life's traffic jams and empty promises
Beating me senseless
Desperation has me on the ropes
I'm still standing, but barely

I'm exhausted and punch drunk
With swollen, puffy eyes
A bloody nose and a fat lip
Threatened by everything
Judging everyone
Deflated by defeat

All this misery has to go somewhere
Either outside or inside
Beating up on myself
Or hating on whoever is handy

But sometimes,
It all goes up in smoke
If I'm lucky
It lands on the paper

Meanwhile
I'm just training for my next surprise bout
Where I'll fight the good fight – again
Bobbing and weaving away from that
Knock-out punch
As long as I can

Mortality Awareness

I am consumed by my mortality awareness
An – I could go at any minute – wariness
Every little ache and pain
Starts the churning in my brain
Fear and worry driving me insane
Former "cure all" now leaves me paranoid
Fearing
The nearing
Death, I can't avoid

I was mourning another colleague when
Mr. Bobdobalina sidled up to me
To flirt and fill me with fear
Told a tale of a woman whose sciatica
Turned out to be a lung tumor!

I felt those words like a gong
Didn't I have back and leg trouble?
Didn't I smoke?
Oh God. . . I'm going to die
Maybe within a month like she did
Oh God, my children...
My husband...
What will they do without me?
Wait

If I'm dead, they are no longer my problem
There will be nothing I can do for them
Hey...all my problems gone....
We could be on to something....
I would never do that to my children
Sometimes I do wonder why I take the slow way
Smoking these cigarettes

But I know we are all gonna die someday
And we don't know when and we don't know where
And it probably won't be fair
Leaving behind a young family
Or undone dreams
Or too many things
Or a legacy
But there is no sense worrying about anything
Cause worry never changed a thing
Que Sera Sera
So even though I'm hyper aware of my
Impending mortality
I have to embrace the reality
That it happens to everyone some time
With depressing normality
Leaving us buried in the finality
Of life
Just an endless struggle to meet one's basic needs
Buoyed by the tiny, fantastic moments in between
The moments full of love
The ones where you just, Go for it.
You just live for your dream

So, you better get busy living
Or get busy dying
But it's hard when my heart is racing
From excitement
And I hear that little voice in my head
That says, "Elizabeth!
This is the big one honey, I'm coming!"

Then I think so what if it's the big one?
I'm going out with a bang!
So the next time I get a pain
It will remind me
I'm still ALIVE

This pain is probably just a sore muscle
From the job or working out
Or maybe it's from my myriad of other conditions
Like varicose veins
Monthly lady pains
Or just plain getting old

Oh, please don't let it be a bedroom injury!
I can't be too old for that

So I'm just gonna keep playing hurt
Thru the mild and frequent aches
And try not to worry,
Since it won't help anyway
I resolve to live every day
Like it's my last
Until my time has passed
Every experience will show on my body
As I refuse to age gracefully
See I have to wear out my body,
Before my mind goes

And I am still grateful for every day above ground
But the worst part of aging
Is the funerals of friends and family
Forcing us to face the fact
That life marches on
Until it doesn't

Salve

Poems are the salve I create
To soothe my wounded soul
Softening the sting of world's painful truths,
Reducing them to a dull ache
That hovers on the edge of my consciousness

Ravings of a Mad Woman

Lady Baby

I am unable
to slam the door
With enough force
to expend my anger!
This product of my loins
Has pushed my buttons again
And I let her --

I swear if Lady Baby doesn't get her face smacked today
It's because I am afraid, I will beat her to death

The self-described "Lady Baby"
Looks like a lady on the outside
But feels like a baby on the inside
She still wants all the rights and privileges
Of an adult
With none of the responsibility

I am exasperated with the
Defiance, laziness, lying and disrespect
And then,
She turns it around on me
Like I'm destroying her self-esteem
By insisting that she finish something!

It's hard to teach someone not to be a
JERKFACE
Clearly, I'm not qualified
The words to describe the audacity of this woman child
Have escaped from my gaping jaw
My eloquence lost to a never-ending battle of wills
All the nurturing has been pushed from my being
By my confounding, contrary Lady Baby

I know sometimes she's just a hormonal mess
Other times she's showing off for her friends,
Provoking me on purpose
But ALL of the time she's a lazy, lying, ungrateful brat
A mendacious little sloth who's sponging off me
I'm embarrassed that I haven't been able to bring her up
Any better than this.

I'm sure it's my fault,
Either my bad parenting
Or my bad genes
Maybe I'm just a middle-aged Mom
Struggling with losing control of my teen
That would suggest I ever had control of that kid
I never have
I'm struggling to be a better person
And a better parent

I'm trying to teach her lessons
She really needs to know
But she thwarts me at every turn
It's about time somebody taught her a lesson
Right upside her idiot head
And knocked some sense into her
Just like it was knocked into me, when I was acting a fool.
Maybe that wasn't sense we got knocked into us
Maybe it was respect.
But I chose not to spank
So now the same hand-wringer who knocked some sense into me
Had the nerve to suggest
We get the kid an acronym diagnosis
With a prescription
And a positive prognosis
All because we can't beat our kids anymore!
The LAST thing I'm gonna do is give that kid
PERMISSION,

An excuse for this bad behavior
A new license to lie and deny

I really do love my lady baby
Although she never makes it easy
Layering her bad behavior on top
Of her arrogant attitude
I've had my fill of sneers and jeers
I'm just sick of her
Put off by my own offspring
I've taken away everything
And nothing works!!

When I treat her the way she DESERVES,
I feel like a jerk
I just don't know what to do anymore
So, I pray every night
That my infuriating, obstinate, selfish,
Pain-in-the-ass Lady Baby
Will one day
grow up to be
An employed, self-sufficient adult
Who has NEVER
Been punched in the face
By her mother.

ANGRY

I woke up angry
In my dirty house
That no one will clean but me
Because that's MY job
Since I'm the Mom
It makes no difference that I work
More hours than anyone else here
The housework, is still mine
Unless I can cajole someone else into
Helping ME with what will
Always be MY job

I woke up angry
In my dirty house
So my face won't smile
And my voice is shrill
At work
I sarcastically suggest
That women be put into
Positions of power
So we can get the work done
Even though he agreed it was a good idea
There aren't any women to put there
Where they will be ignored by the men
Because they have a pissing contest to sustain
They have to measure their dicks every day
So you can be sure they are still dicks
Every day

I swear to the good Lord
I am so ANGRY
I am ready to run for Congress
Privacy be damned
My life is an open book

No amount of embarrassment
About things men do
DAILY
Will keep me out of the ring
Maybe I was a slut in college
So what?
Maybe I took some drugs to escape
The pain of this man's world
So what?
Crucify me for standing up for women
Go ahead!
Do your worst!
Dox me
I don't care
So what?
I woke up angry
And I'm not alone

There will come a time
When you can no longer
Shame us
Or silence us
Or belittle us
Or ignore us

We will take our power
Then WE – women
Will make sure everyone has health care
Education, food, shelter and clean water
I am so perplexed by Christians
Who DON'T want that for everyone else
Do you really think that is what Jesus would do?

I know THAT is taking the Lord's name in vain
When you choose the money changers
Over the poor, the sick, the forgotten
You spit in the eye of the Lord
You are not one of his followers
You are a wolf in sheep's clothing
Waiting to pounce on the weak

Just get ready for the meek
to inherit the world
Because we – women
The formerly weak
Are ANGRY
Very, very ANGRY
#metoo & #timesup
And we will take action
See you in Washington!

Pains

Now men are saying
That menstrual cramps are all in our heads
Ha Ha Ha
That's a good one
Because it never happens to them
It never happens at all
They don't want us to have our own feelings
Or our own needs
Because then we can't focus on THEIR
Feelings and needs

I wish I could make men spend
An entire day in a pair of control-top panty-hose
That are 2 sizes too small
Maybe I could punch each one in the stomach
10 times a day
Or let me tie a huge rope
Around your middle
Then twist it tighter & tighter & tighter

Then you tell me how much it doesn't hurt
I'm sure it wouldn't hurt you
Because you're so tough and macho
Because you wouldn't squeal like a little girl
If you found a crime scene in your pants
Or your bed or in the shower
And don't forget somebody has to clean up that mess
So YOU won't be traumatized
By remembering that I bleed
EVERY MONTH I'M NOT IMPREGNATED

It's gross and nasty
But it shouldn't be
It's natural
It's healthy
It means we're fertile
But it still hurts
And sometimes it makes me sad
The moon controls my cycle
It strips away the softness
Protecting me from the world's hard truths

The weight of the world
Is heavier than usual
Eroding my skin
Leaving my nerves raw and exposed
Leaving me weary and irritable
On top of all these cramps.
They feel like the start
Of labor
It is my body laboring to expel the excess

(Lamaze breathing)
Strap in because this is the tough part
Where I use my taxed protection products
Sometimes all of them at once
Take some more meds
Do more Lamaze breathing
And I CARRY ON

While some people have the nerve
To claim that cramps don't even exist
This insult to women
Is why we need comprehensive health education
And comprehensive health care
And Adoption of the idea
That Women Are People

Not just servants
And maids
And pretty decorations
Not just receptacles for your sperm
Not just incubators for your offspring

We are whole entire people
Each woman is a person
With the rights to her own
Thoughts, feelings and body
I wish that was the reality
While my body is angry with me
For not bearing fruit
Somehow when I don't add to the world
Its problems become mine
But while I'm suffering,
Remind me to smile at you
So you feel OK.

Lazy

I have been a hard worker
My entire life
And still called lazy
I couldn't sit in front of the TV
As a child
Without being given
A bowl of beans to snap
Or butter beans to shell
Or laundry to fold
Or clothes to iron
Or something to sort
Or something to clean
Seldom was I allowed to sit idle
I would surely be called lazy
Or bookworm
Which I prefer
Reading was an escape
I could get away with
Especially if I finished all the chores

I grew up in a culture
Of accountability
If you were assigned a job
You did it
Or you were punished
Or you couldn't leave
Until your chores were finished
Not doing the chores
Just wasn't an option

After being held accountable
My entire life
I now hold myself accountable
If I say I will do it
I will
Or I will give it my best shot

So, I expect when you say
You will do something
You will
It's called accountability
And it causes integrity

It's just that simple
Especially at work
Since that is literally
Your job

In order to work together
We need to hold each other accountable
You agreed to be responsible
For this item
Now you only have excuses
Worse than that
All the other fellows
Circle the wagons around you
Protecting you from
The big bad lady
Asking you how and when
You are going to have that ready?

If you guys aren't having a pissing contest
To mark your territory,
You are sniffing each other's butts
And protecting your precious pack
From any and all accountability
Seriously
Why are you even here?
If we are not all trying to move this forward together?

In order to move,
We have to take steps
And the first ones are
Completing the tasks
As outlined in the list you demanded
But you didn't like the list
that was too specific
too many concrete things
TO ACTUALLY DO

growing up in a house of all girls
there was no man to do
man jobs
so I did them

my hard work
was praised
and I was raised to believe
I could do anything
I wanted
right after I did
whatever they wanted

that I could be anything I wanted
except man things
who wanted to do that anyway?

I hate working in a man's world
I really do
I am just here to get the job done
But you hate it when I'm good at anything
You spend precious time
we could be working
Plotting against me
or looking up my skirt
I have the answers to all your problems,
But no one will listen to me
Being here is just exhausting
Why am I even existing here?
Why won't they let me be great?

Paralyzed by poverty

Paralyzed by poverty
Into inaction
But there are so many things to do
And I can't afford to do them
Or not to do them
But I don't have the proper tools
Or knowledge
And I can't pay anyone
Who does

So here I sit
With tasks, troubles and traumas
Piling up around me
Overwhelming me
But I just can't move
Can't even cry out for help
That I know isn't there
I just don't know what to do
I feel so useless
So helpless
So worthless
Trapped in this poverty

What I need to do
I don't want to
Like take these dishes
And wash them in the bathtub
Because the kitchen sink
Won't drain
Our homemade fixes
Can't touch the elixir
Of mire that lurks
In our pipes
Threatening to blow back

Into our living space
Maybe it already has
I know I feel like I'm covered in it

Every single thing costs money
Money that I don't have
Money that hasn't arrived yet
It's so degrading to live like this
In a broken-down house
I can't afford to fix
I am lucky just to make the payments
Society tells me I'm poor
Because of my poor choices
That I deserve this
That I'm worthless
And I'm starting to believe them
I just can't stand this

It sucks to be this broke
I try not to live check to check
But last time I checked
Alternatives were suspect
Every single time I dig out of the hole
I feel a little bit like I have control
some breathing room,
a tragedy befalls me
and you can bet it costs
all my money

no matter how hard I work
no matter how smart I am
no matter what I choose
I always lose
I always lose

All Natural

Starry night at Nana's

The starriest spot in the vast night sky
That I've ever seen
Is above my mother's house
Not even the mature trees
Can block the magnitude of the sky there
With a multitude of brilliant polka dots
Dancing in 3-D darkness

I have never seen so many stars before
In my life
Much less in one place
Maybe I never went into the dark, to see them
my mother lives in the country
where it's dark without street lights and shopping malls
The night is quiet, pleasant, and inviting
Prompting me to work on my moon tan

There is little phone service out here
Preserving the integrity of the blackness
Allowing me to lie back
And just watch the show

Each star is an idea beckoning me
I refuel on the twinkling tranquility
Staring at the starry wonder,
My eyes relax
My mind starts to wander
Around
In the world I have created for myself
Among the stars

I am drifting so far

Harshly jolted back to reality
By my mother asking
"What are you doing out here?"

"Just looking at the stars," I answer
Pinning my dreams on them, I think
Smiling because I don't tell her that part
I'm afraid she can't see what I see
In the sky
Or in me

The Write Beach

On this visit to the sea
I decided NOT to read on the beach
This is a big deal
As I love to read
And I never have time
Except on vacation

No, this trip, I will only write
But first I will look
At the ocean
I will listen to it
I will just be

And relax into being
Letting thoughts come to me unbidden
They are random

But when I am writing
I am not looking
Not living
But recording that living
So that moments may endure time

I will watch and
I will write
I will paint rolling waves
With words that
Splash onto the paper

I will try to explain how
By never stopping
The waves represent life
They keep crashing to the shore
No matter what happens

It is soothing to watch the waves
Just the way it should be soothing
To know that life will go on

But reality relentlessly crashing
Onto my shores
Is eroding me
The ravages of circumstance
Washing me away

And I long for a sunny day
With a lounge chair,
And a cocktail,
And a pile of (paid) bills,
But even with none of that

On a cloudy day
Sitting on a towel on the sand
At the edge of the continent
Watching the shore get pummeled
By the waves

I still find it soothing
Just as soothing as aloe vera gel
Will be on my sunburn

The ocean's relief is also fleeting,
Just like the aloe
So, re-apply as often as you can.

Cloudy

It's been cloudy
nearly this whole beach trip

Thunderstorms were forecast
But what we have is overcast

Overcast always makes me think
Someone hired too many actors
For the part of cloud

Now they are obscuring the star

Or maybe they hired one huge actor
To do a tiny bit part
Who is now chewing up the scenery

That is overcast

That is probably the cloud with the thunderstorm
The big one
Showing off dazzling lightning bolts
And its dark underside

You cloud, mind your manners

We sun worshipers don't mind a bit of respite
Under your haze

But you could stop spitting at me
I don't care if I get wet,
This is the beach
But you are getting the pages wet

As if to thwart my attempt to capture you
And take you home with me

But I will take back enough
Ocean, sand and sky
To last me until next year

Date Night

I want you so badly, I can hardly bear it.

It started innocently enough
The sunlight glinting off your hair
Ignited a fire inside of me

The two of us basking in the surf
Lying together on the sand
The sun's rays caressing our skin
With a gentle touch
We will later imitate
Starting the slow burn
That would last
All
Through
The
Night

Over dinner your eyes undressed me
Uncovering my need for your touch
I pretended my dessert was you
Playfully teasing it into my mouth
Savoring every last morsel
Our swaying bodies melding into one
The dancing was just practice
So we could get our steps together

Later we walk hand in hand
Down the deserted beach
Mooning over each other
Watching the moon over the ocean
Grateful for this week of moments
Together

Apart from everything that
Comes between us
We come together
Delighting in a moonlight stroll
Bathing in the warm, gentle surf
Recreating
Famous frolics in the froth
We make our own film
For only the gods to see

Dawn

I watch the sky transform itself
Into the tangerine dream of sunrise
Slowly launching up from the ocean
Under a fingernail moon and a planet sentry
The sky is aflame with possibilities

I stare as if in a trance
Memorizing
This dawn's advance
Colors streaming
Across the vast expanse
of a sky
Wide open
Filled with sustenance
Foreshadowing another sunny scorcher

I paint it in my mind like Bob Ross
Where happy little clouds dance across the heavens
With highlights of hot pink dawning into light orange
Over a calming, blue sea
The bigger waves, not yet awake
Color trinity hinting at a new day

Dawn casts an angelic light on the clouds
As if the underside were holy
A ship slowly eclipses the glowing pink orb
Revealing just the soft round fringe
Peeking over the edge
of the planet

What once felt so close
Like a show only for me
Has sailed away
To the very edge of the world
Just past the sea
Filling the horizon with promise

I am enthralled with the dawn

I devour the scene
Drinking it in with my eyes
Tattooing it onto my soul
Letting this tranquility
Permeate every cell of my being
creating an impression
of this moment
on my psyche
So I can visit this peaceful
palace any time I need to

Icy

The shock of the cold ocean water
baptizing me in the notion
The waves are life
Building the tension, the suspense
The crashing
Dumping bits of sand back on the beach

How you handle the waves is up to you
Jump up
Dive under
Swim out past the break

As long as you remember
The awesome power of the waves
Driven by the moon

Beware the undertow
Drawing you into the sea
Like a sacrifice to the inevitableness
That IS life
When it seems like there are more downs than ups

Remember that moment
When you were a part of the
Majestic power of the sea

Reborn into a new life
Awash in the power of the ocean
Power that lives inside me
If I'm not afraid to use it

If I'm not afraid to surf
The rough waters of life
And try to ride on top
If I am not afraid
I will use my power
I will be OK

I will ride the waves
Until I can finally
Propel myself out past the break
And all the time
I will be OK
Because I have the power

And so do you
Because it was born
Into all of us
If only
You are not afraid to use it

So dive into the icy, cold waters
Unafraid.
Bathe in your own power
Become one with the world
Ride the oceans waves
Like a friendly tide washing
You back home
Because you belong here

We have been waiting for you

How did I get here?

Pineapple

I want to write like a pineapple
rather than a bitter star fruit
I hold my crown erect
but you can elect to
look past my spiny exterior
designed to protect
and deflect
rejection
My prickly skin
covers my sweet, juicy insides
where my words are
delicate, delicious flesh
delivering fresh
nourishment
Grown from my tough core
allowing me to weave my fibers
into a yarn, so complex
you taste both the sour and the sweet

Beautiful Disaster

I'm at my most beautiful
When I don't care how I look
When it looks effortless
(Because I spent no effort)
To beautify my outside
Because I KNOW
The light inside me
Brightens my skin
When my confidence radiates through every pore
Creating a flawless foundation

Washed away by my salty tears

All the Jenga blocks of my existence
That were once artfully stacked
Have come crashing down
Into a puddle of disarray
And I am misery

Complete and total destruction
I will never be able to reconstruct them
The way they once were
For every tumbling of the tower takes its toll
People keep taking my blocks
So, I will never feel whole
Until I use the blocks to build a better foundation
One that doesn't rely on appearance
But is so sturdy, it's stunning
And is so strong and so stable
It ceases to be a tower
But instead becomes a table
Set for mine enemies

To feed, heal and care for them
So, they might climb my stairs
To the launching pad there
Where people start to chase their dreams

but it seems
that there's been an accident
Smashed by a distracted driver
Crashed into my foundation
Jolting my whole world
With the force of an earthquake
in
just
one
second
And I am in trouble
Once again reduced to rubble
But I will always rebuild
With whatever I learned in the last crash
As both fuel and mortar
Pushing me past
Where I used to be
I will make my new table broader
So more can dine with me
Because I will always believe
That love trumps hate
And that would make this disaster
Beautiful—Again

Energy

How do you have so much energy?
They ask me
And I say
How do you sit quietly?
I'd like to know because ADHD
With a side of Endometriosis
Is my self-diagnosis
It really explains everything
Like how to make a mountain
Out of every molehill
Because I have 99 problems
And I am 98 of them
Like forbidden fruit
I wish I still ate of them
Because I'm starving
But I can't make myself eat
Everything tastes like defeat
It's not giving me what I need

If you start with a 100 percent
And subtract my 98
You're left with 2
Which is my perfect number
Because I am too hot
Unless I am too cold
I feel both
Too young
And too old
Too timid and
Too bold
Too apt to scold
Because everything is too loud

Or too quiet
Too boring
Or brewing into a riot

Wearing my nerves outside my skin
The sensitivity overload sets in
Or sets off
All my detectors
I knew it was going to be a bad day
When my clothes hurt my skin
Which is uncomfortable to be in
All my graciousness has left me
Returned itself to heaven
While my emotions are dialed up to 11
With no buffer
Need a fluffer
But please don't touch me
My skin can't bear it
But I need to be hugged
Even when it hurts

When the extravert
Needs to be alone
It feels like we are disappointing
Those we are usually annoying
With our constant chatter

Instead
Let the words flow through me
Soothing my sensitivity
Channeling my energy
Positively
So that I might exist
Painlessly
And vibrate all of my energy
At a higher frequency

Recovery

The few, fleeting images before my lost time,
Might have suggested an alien abduction
My bed was wheeled by windows
As if this should be my final glimpse of blue sky
Clad only in a flimsy gown
And a silly, silver hat
I am soon surrounded by a small, masked army
In blue scrubs and shower caps

One of them makes me list the things the aliens are going to do to me
To make sure I know
To make sure I consent
Maybe one of them is a lawyer
She assures me, though,
They know exactly what they are going to do to me
She takes my glasses
My arms are tied down
And covered with warm, heavy blankets
A mask covers my nose and mouth
Down the hall I hear someone say
"Think of your favorite vacation spot"
And I am at the beach
For about 3 seconds...
Then the lights go out

I remember nothing from having my consternation removed
Tiny bombs of pain were disengaged before they could
Explode their crippling misery upon me

But I know something has been removed
I can feel it in every movement
That something was taken out of me.
I can feel it in every step I take
I feel like a vase that's just been re-glued

So fragile, any little bump or jar
Could destroy the whole thing
I would collapse in a pile of pieces
This improvement has left me feeling broken
So, I tread lightly and carefully
Just until it starts to hurt
From where they cut through the casual veneer
Of ease and confidence that protects me
Forming my skin
Cutting through every layer of my self
All the way down to my very core
To excise the part that is destroying me
Incisions allowing my power, my energy
And my light—to leave me
Leaving me tired, achy and sore

I can feel my body trying to fuse itself
Back together
To weave a new layer of strength over my core
To safely harness my power
Building an repairing my internal support system
With REST
Persistent aches and pains in my abdomen
Say "You're not quite whole again"
While itchy stitches can barely hold my light in
So must rest until I am stronger
I am not ready to give any light away

This poem took a long time coming to me
Like that first dump after surgery
It couldn't find its way through the codeine haze
Or my Swiss cheese torso maze

I miss my old self
I miss my energy
I feel like an old lady

With all this convalescing
I didn't know being in the world
Took so much out of me
The light and love I gave so freely
Has nearly seeped all the way out of me
Through the tiny holes left in me
And my weary recovery
While still itchy stitches can barely hold my light in
So, I must rest until I am stronger
Until my light is so bright again
It can't be hidden
And it comes unbidden
To revive the bedridden
But until then

You can find me under my bushel,
No
I'm not gonna let it shine;
When I'm recovered and feeling fine
Then, I'm gonna let it shine
Let it shine
Let it shine
Let it shine

I Know Things

I know things

Things about me
And things about you

Although they are unsaid
I feel that they are true
That's how the vibrations do

I know things

Before they happen
I can see the future

Hear it whisper in my ear
But don't worry
No one ever listens to me

If they do
They don't believe

But that will never make my vision
Any less true
Because I know things

Things about me
And things about you

Hunter

I was born to be a hunter
My mind moves at cheetah speed
Like my eyes
Scanning
Keeping watch
I have poor eyesight
But an eagle eye
No movement goes unnoticed
No sound goes unidentified
Each gets categorized
And echolocated
Instantly

And you think I'm not paying attention
But I don't miss anything
And I feel everything
I am so sensitive
I can detect slight changes
in temperature
And energy
My bloodhound nose
can detect a whiff of contempt
From across the room
When I sense danger
Or prey
Every hair stands on end
Enlarging me
Energizing me
Preparing me
To slay the beast
My body becomes a spring
And I am coiled tight
Ready to pounce
Ready to destroy the enemy

Protecting my tribe
And bringing home the bacon

And you are upset because I can't sit still
Of course, I can't sit still
I wasn't meant to
When I am forced to
I can't engage
And boredom
Sets in
That's when the real trouble begins
I start seeking stimulation
Barreling toward disruption
Either from entertaining my neighbors
Or some tapping, clicking, fidgeting
Wiggling, giggling
Just do the work you insist
But I'm already finished
I told you my mind moves at cheetah speed
Maybe if you just let me read
Until the others catch up

You call me lazy
But you have no idea
That my imagination is working over time
Processing all the stimuli around me
Into art or poetry
I can focus intently
On something that stimulates me

Nope, I only get chiding
Telling me I'm not living up to my potential
Because you want me to progress neatly
Marching in a line like everyone else
But I can't
My life doesn't move linearly

My life is in 3D
I'm not reaching my potential
Because you keep limiting me

Most of my natural hunter instincts
Can be tamed with arts and activity
But don't label me with ADHD
And fix me with medication
To fit your idea of education
Under constant condemnation
Cause I can't stay in formation
And no amount of dedication
On my part can help
Why can't I learn in my way?
Because my brain moves at cheetah speed
Why can't you keep up with my needs?

But no, I'm the one who's broken
Not the system
That's not prepared for hunters
Not prepared for my level of activity
Not equipped for someone sensitive like me
Because every slight is magnified
And could traumatize
And stigmatize
My gifts
As not right
Something to be corrected
So I can be connected
A part of the group
But that's not my way

I'm atypical
I'm different
Because I was born to be a hunter
My mind moves at cheetah speed

Monster Under Your Bed

The truth is a hideous monster
hiding under your bed
The one they said
Was all in your head
But you
gave form to that nagging dread

You didn't listen when they insist
Monsters don't exist
Even so, you know
The Truth does persist
And you are powerless to resist

Because you know it's there
You can sense it's beady-eyed stare
You feel the graze of its hair
Its putrid stench defiling the air
Waiting, seething in its lair
Under its withering glare
All your phobias are laid bare
Go forth, if you dare
It's inescapable
It's everywhere

What if it's not a monster at all?
Only a foreboding you cannot name
It is simply Truth
Your fear has made it grotesque
The unknown, a horror burlesque
Afraid you'll be its next conquest
But this is not a contest
Only an illusion
You did manifest

Between yourself and the beast
It is a creature of your own making
While everyone thinks you are faking
Your own heart, you're staking
Truth waits there, for the taking
From the nightmare you are finally waking

Old dangers fade away
When you utter
The words you are afraid to say
The ideas you are afraid to embrace
Panic and terror, they will replace
Filling you with unending grace
As fear disappears without a trace

Then, it can once again, be your friend
Let the Truth take you by the hand
And lead you past pitfalls of quicksand
Over your worries, tiny and grand
Holding you, until you learn to stand
There
you will find
The promised land

Electricity

The electricity between us is
Visible to the naked eye
And I'm afraid someone might see
Cuz your third eye penetrates mine
Inviting my soul to intertwine
Tempting me to dine
On your soul food

Your intoxicating scent
Sends tingles up my spine
My word, you are divine
I've spent too much time
With these pictures in my mind
Where you flex my spine
But they serve to remind
Me, that my
Fading fertility is on fleek
Feeling my pheromones
Floating freely from me
forming forces far larger
than just you and me
Making me wary
of your proximity

Because the electricity between us
Is magnetic
I am so drawn to you
That I can barely look at you
Afraid our eyes will lock
Exposing my desire
So, I quickly turn around
Facing my opposite pole
Toward you
In an effort to repel you

So I am not trapped in your field
Of sexually charged ions
Believe me, I got my eyes on you
I don't want to adhere myself to you
I mean
I do
You got me by the ovary
I wanna have your baby
Not really, just practice
A miracle of prophylactics
But I'm afraid the attraction
Will become an attachment
And we are both too married for that ish
Damn my continued ovulation
Sending reason to obscurity
Searching for my maturity
To uphold my fidelity

Because the electricity
Between us is visible
To the naked eye
And I
Can't deny
I want to be naked with you
But I wasn't trying to tell you
About it

So, I beg you,
Please
Don't stand so close to me

Mediocre Poem

Shout out to the mediocre poem
The ones that refuse to be revised
Cutting out any words
Feels like telling lies
It defies
Reduction
Contrary to all instruction
But telling it straight
Devoid of seduction
Causes the introduction
Of boredom
Correct in your deduction
The sound you hear is suction
Vacuuming interest
Right out of the room

But I can't quit you
Because each mundane part
Touches another's tortured heart
Even if the poem seems too long
And you wish it would retire
But the pressure never relents
Even when you tire of it

I know the perfect piece is in there
But it's not ready yet
It will be a Frankenstein masterpiece
Cobbled together from the best bits
Of the least of these
Mediocre poems

Manifest

My countenance
Is due to my competence
Coupled with my confidence
You can count on this
watch me manifest
Cuz I can manifest
My destiny
On stages from L.A. to Schenectady
And even in Texas
Imma be bigger than Texas
Watch me flex this
'Cause I'm the nexus
And I know what's next is
Meant only for me
What is meant for you,
Is meant only for you
No one can take that away from you

So, if you can dream it
and you can believe it
and you can see it
and write it
and speak it

You. Can. Be. It.
You can make it happen
Would that
Make you happy?

Don't Tread on Me Either

5th of July

The hot, humid air smelled smoky
I looked around for a fire burning
I knew it was in men's hearts
The fire for triumph over tyranny
And the celebration of
Imaginary victories
With masturbatory fireworks
A flash fire reminder of war
Dressed up in its Sunday best
And trotted out on parade
So we can say we are the best
Country in the world

But let's really Be Best
Put our faith to the test
Put aside our pseudo-weapons
To break bread with our neighbors
And unite against the tyranny
That is our collective enemy

A Tale of Two Dons

Thin-skinned bullies
Manipulative crybabies
Shameless jerks
Looking out for number one
Lie, cheat and steal to get what they want
Won't be held accountable
Not their fault
You made them do it
Your nagging
Your constant pushing them to be decent
Forced them to lash out even harder
No one else's wants, needs or feelings matter
Unless they can be used to the Dons' advantage
Ruthless savage
their brutal behavior has world
wishing for their comeuppance

Greedily gobbling up all the resources
They have no intention of working for
Won't pull their considerable weight
Don't try to take the spotlight away from them
Their petty egos can't take it
So they switch on the charm
And dial it up to 11
You forget what a terror the Don is
You remember how much fun the Don is
And why you fell in love in the first place

The second your eyes get dreamy
Don goes in for the kill
Pulling the rug out from under you
Once again
Starting a new imaginary fight
Or rehashing a settled issue

They lost on
You're left battered and confused
What just happened here?

It was a drive-by drama
The kind used by drama farmers
To start just a little something new
To plant a seed of doubt
With a well-placed put-down

Dons love to use this hit and run
Keeps the enemy (you) off balance
"But I am not the enemy"
You scream.
"I love Don"
Ah, but to the two Dons
You are the enemy
Insisting they have integrity
And treat you with respect
Because you accept nothing less
You have become
The enemy
And you know what Dons
Do to their enemies,
Right?

Make them offers they can't refuse.

Colorblind

Our Pavlov's head continues to swell
As he rings the Twitter bell
Turning the news hounds
Into lap dogs
Lap, lap, lapping up vitriol and hate
Regurgitating it as yellow journalism all over us.
24-hour coverage and analysis of
An Orange attention whore
Modern-day minstrel
Playing the media like a fiddle every day
And the news cycle junkies just can't wait
For another hit.
Just because it's in black and white
And read all over doesn't make it news

Let's see what the clown will do today
Titillate us, make us gasp
Force feed us Entertainment and call it information
Any distraction so we don't fall into formation
And realize the causation of our distress
Keep us focused on the 3 rings in front of us
This is the very definition of a circus

Just outside the spotlight
The one man trying to turn it around
Speaks truth into a video void
Major media outlets carefully avoid
Covering the one talking sense
In favor of sensationalism

All the showman wants is your attention
He'll do anything to get it
This is the biggest show ever
The ratings are irrelevant

It doesn't matter what you say about him,
As long as you keep saying his name
So you can't #SAYHERNAME
He cares about nothing except his own fame
Gifted with a purple heart
It's faded to lavender
when pinned to the chest of a lily-livered coward
A flailing bully lashing out at all challengers
Playground name-calling
And blue language NOT
Befitting a leader

He's a gold medal hype man
Plated with the crappiest fool's gold
Russian money can buy
A cheap, shiny bauble
Bombastic
Practically plastic
Morals of elastic
Distracting you
From the solutions to our problems

If you can't see his true colors
You are every kind of blind & deaf & dumb
Clinging to white supremacy can only lead
To our demise
Humans are one race of people
Best led by those who are Wise
Decent and Kind
and want to strengthen our union
Not destroy it.

Tales of a 4th Grade Nothing: Presidential Edition

"I'm rubber and you're glue
Everything you say,
Bounces off of me
And sticks to you!"
Is the philosophy of this administration

They say everyone else is lying
Because everything they say is a lie
Every single lie they told on anyone else
Is true of them
They think protesters are paid
Because they paid all of theirs

They fear restroom interactions
Because of their predatory bathroom behavior
They insist there was voter fraud
That one is actually true
They know, because THEY committed it.

They fear anyone who is different from them
Since they are greedy, wicked and cruel
They assume everyone else is greedy, wicked and cruel

Then they try to scare us with those "others'
While they rob us blind
And blame the others

"Fake news" is the lies and BS that they tell us
While claiming anyone telling a truth they don't like is
...fake news
They prize loyalty above all else
That's the "honor among thieves"
You've heard tell of

Whined about Obama's vacations
Golfs every weekend
Complains about wasteful government spending
Costs us a fortune in security detail

Buy American, Hire American
Uses foreign workers to build with Chinese steel

U.S. has a military larger than most
All others – combined
Wants to beef up the military
Enriching his contractor pals
Stiffing Veterans, again.

Cried and cried about emails
Uses private unsecured devices daily
Pence gets hacked NBD

Every time some truth escapes,
They blame the leaker
Unless it's the Leaker-in-Chief
Constantly contradicting lying spokesmen
Trying to save his ass
Because he's PROUD of his debauchery

His mastery of Orwellian doublespeak
Is impressive
Since we can be sure he never read it
This pompous, purveyor of word salad
Speaks on a 4th grade level
Because that's his command of the language
Boasts of hoards who love him
Because he is lonely, needy, hated and sad

It's just sad
Really, just sad
Bigly sad
And covfefe

Tales of a 4th grade Nothing: Presidential Edition

Blame

I blame OJ for the 24-hour news cycle,
That Bronco drove us to insanity

I blame Hugh Heffner for dirty old men in open bathrobes, worldwide
I blame White Supremacy for dividing us
I blame churches for not bringing us back together
I blame corporations for destroying our environment
I blame the government for their complicity in our detriment
I blame climate deniers for our accelerating demise

I blame the greedy for homelessness
I blame those with abundance for starvation
I blame all of us for our alienation from each other
I blame the traffic on lousy public transportation
I blame sexism for idiot men getting promoted over brilliant women

I blame myself for never being good enough
I blame my family for the chores they ignore
I blame my mom for making me feel guilty and fat
I blame my dad for leaving us
I blame my misery on everyone but me
I blame the endometriosis for my monthly mood disorder
I blame the government for obscuring the cure
I blame the well-meaning, well-to-do for failing to legislatively
    help the poor.
I blame the rich for destroying the middle class
I blame Faux News and Gerry Mandering for Trump

I blame us all for not loving each other
I blame us all for not coming together and taking back our government
    for the people
I blame myself for not doing more, than trying to write the poem that
    saves the world.

Becky Disguise

I wear this Becky disguise
So you don't realize
I'm passing
Until it's too late
And you discover I am a diploma
A dental plan, and
A few blocks away
From being White Trash
I know I'm lucky to live adjacent to Trump Town
And not in it
But for my own safety, I have to blend
You didn't expect to hear
the truth to come from here
I am not as docile, as I appear

That's right, I'm a radical,
a lefty liberal
And a socialist
But I don't look it
See maybe if I don't look threatening
My ideas won't frighten you

I'm just your Basic Becky
Or Business Barbie over here
Nothing to fear
So it's safe for you to hear
What I have to tell you

The truth is
Revolution is near
I can feel the unease
Swirling around me
The storm is picking up speed
It is time for the unrich

To stand together
Forming a flood wall
That protects the small
We will direct the torrent of anger
At our oppressors
As soon as we wake up
And see who they are
A lot of names followed by
the letter R

Don't be fooled
If your oppressor looks like you
Or even like me
He's still deceiving you
Stealing your money
And blaming others
Your growth he smothers
Taking the gains
For HIS family
Leaving little
For you and me
To fight over
futilely
Cause when we are divided
we will never have enough
But together we can shake things up

Rise up together
Against tyranny
And be free

How to grow a terrorist

1. Pick a group and marginalize them, for centuries.
2. Trap them in ghettos with no transportation, healthy food or jobs.
3. Deny the marginalized access to education, clean water, and opportunity.
4. Make sure other citizens unreasonably fear the marginalized group.
5. Allow Peace Officers to murder the marginalized in the streets without reason, punishment or accountability.
6. Allow other citizens to murder them. Take away the assailants armor-covered, upright body for all to see.
7. Steal all their shoes, and burn down the boot factory. Blame the barefoot for failing to pull themselves up by their bootstraps.
8. If someone from the marginalized group is widely elected by a large group of citizens, attack relentlessly. Cause a huge decisive rift, and then blame that leader for dividing us.
9. If anyone from the marginalized group kills another within their own group, again blame them and use it as an excuse to fear and kill them.
10. Mock them in the face of their peaceful protest.
11. Constantly fuel the fires of hate with guilt from the sins of your fathers.
12. Call yourself a Christian, fearing and loathing all who do not, but never act in a Christ-like way.
13. Get so accustomed to your privilege and entitlement that justice seems unfair to you.
14. Run around screaming "The sky is falling, the sky is falling," but never take responsibility for chopping down its pillars.
15. Now that you have stolen their joy, their hope, and incarcerated their children, stand back and wait and watch.

Imma find a place to hide because no one will ever be safe from the terrorists we created. We sewed a lot of Hate seeds, and we've got a bumper crop coming in.

So mark yourself as a target with a rebel flag across your back and don't forget to, get the fuck over it.

Kum ba ya and such

PRO-LIFE

The reason we can't have Universal Health Care in this country
is because we will not extend personhood
to black, brown, and poor people.

But corporations have personhood
So much so, they can speak
Instead of the people
When money counts as speech
And they've stolen it from each
And every one of us
It's going to take all of us
To claw it back from them

Every single person has value
And deserves healthcare
THAT is what Pro-Life means to me
Pro-Life is not throwing away young lives in prison
Pro-Life is not letting corporations pollute our water
No, Pro-Life protects the air and water FOR THE PEOPLE, all the people
Pro-Life is funding Meals on Wheels
Pro-Life is Healthcare for people, NOT for profit
Pro-Life is housing the homeless
Pro-Life is giving free lunch to school children
Pro-Life is valuing people and families, all of them
Pro-Life is paying workers a living wage
Pro-Life is stricter gun laws
Pro-Life is not executing people

So how long are we going to listen
To this BS about Family Values
When struggling families are vilified, not aided
Their Pro-Life is only Pro-Birth
NOT Pro-Life
With no housing support, no childcare, no food stamps?

That is a pro-prison pipeline
That is its purpose
They are keeping us down, on purpose
Their deceit is wrapped in the flag
And sitting on top of the Bible
Where it is libel to fool some people
Into thinking the thieves are helping them

I can promise you
Nothing they do
Is Pro-Life

They reject anything for the common good
Preferring their personal good
To giving everyone equal personhood
Their Christianity is a falsehood

So if you believe in life
You should demand support for the lives of ALL people
Not just the ones like you
What you don't realize is,
All the people who seem not like you
Have much more in common with you
Than you have in common with the rich

So let's all try to be Pro-Life
Pro the lives of each other
And not fear each other
Try to connect
So we can correct
The inequalities and injustice in our country
That is radically Pro-Life

Patient

You gotta be patient
To be a patient in this country
No one asks about your injury
Until AFTER all the data entry
Naming the financially responsible party
That is key
After we have named who will pay
Then you sign your life away
And consent to whatever they say

So they can ply you with their lethal medications
That only cause dangerous complications
Where treatment for your condition
Is an expensive prescription
And a pre-existing contradiction

Because healing is not a business
It's an art
With a healthy dose of science
And a whole lot of heart
But we have trouble getting to that part
Till we find out who pays
Because the treatment facility
Is not a charity
Or a non-profit
So you only get treatments
That are covered
at a profit

Navigating the pot-holed highways
Of insurance detours requires
Waaaay too much time --
Time I need to rest and heal
And go to the doctor

Yet I have to fight to get my health care
Paid for
And I'm still waiting
To feel cared for

I wish we all cared for each other enough
To DEMAND Single Payer Health Care
I wish we just said NO MORE
To the hassles and denials
Of the insurance companies profiting
Off of our suffering
While simultaneously causing
More suffering
Instead of a Health Care System
We need a Healing System
With an army of helpers

We need
Social workers, doctors, nurses, teachers,
First responders and peace officers
the whole community
Every community in America
To decide
That we are PRO-LIFE enough
To care
about the lives of other people
Prove to me that you believe
That "ALL Lives Matter"
Enough
For health care

I reject your "family values"
that don't value all families
Every single human alive
deserves medical care
We can have

Universal Health Care – Medicare for All
If corporations pay their share and
Invest in a healthy workforce
Instead of providing "insurance"

Don't let them tell you it will cost too much
Overstand
That it offers too much
To the people
Feelings of equality and solidarity,
Dignity and Unity
Employees are free
To change companies
Or start their own
The savings of time alone
Is worth millions

More-efficient, life-saving care
can be had at a fraction
of the current cost

Oh, there is that loss of profit...
For shareholders
All of whom, need healthcare
Just like you

Here you expected
You were gonna be protected
After your premiums were collected
But your claim was rejected
Leaving you neglected
But insurance revenues protected
Cause they bankroll the elected
So, We the Patients need to get connected
So come November, they are ejected
And new leaders are selected

By the people, they are directed
So Health Care can be corrected
And everyone can be expected
To live a long, healthy life

But it will take all families, coming together
Demanding healthcare for each other
Because together we ARE
WE THE PEOPLE
Demanding Healthcare for All
Because we are sick of being patient.

Weary

She said, "You look tired."
"I'm past tired, I'm weary"
So weary of a world that only values
Wealthy, white men
Who clutch their money and power so tightly,
It chokes the rest of us
I'm weary of working just to pay the bills and
Wondering is this all there is?
While my black and brown neighbors cry out
"Just let me live"

I'm weary of the shit always rolling downhill
Polluting the poor neighborhoods
I'm weary of black people getting murdered by police
I am weary of a world that attacks women for everything
Too smart, too dumb, too opinionated, too slutty,
Too covered up, too meek, too frumpy,
Too fat, too thin, too tired of this shit to care
I am weary of the attacks on the only qualified candidate we had left
Just because she had the nerve to act like she belonged there.
Weary of non-PC internet posts being a fireable office
When rape and murder are not.
Weary of complaints about protests and
No WILL to fix the problems
I am weary of inequality and injustice

Weary of robber baron, scam artists vying for the White House
Weary of webs of lies and deceit
Weary of 10 corporations that own everything
Weary of the poor being blamed for their condition
Weary of people dying because they can't afford health care
Weary of scared little bullies lashing out at those who are different
Weary of the disconnect between people

I am weary of a world in which I am wary
Of those who told me to fear others
I am weary of always being other
Until they need me
Then I'm back in the fold
To be imprisoned on a pedestal
I'm welcome to stay....
  In my place
Keeping my head down
And fix a smile on my face
A Stepford-wife model of charm and grace
A credit to my race
Until.... I open my big, liberal mouth
Now I have outed myself
As a believer
In love, truth and justice
The kindness
Of human-kind

But I am weary of being led
By those of a different mind
I am weary of the fearful using religion
As an exclusive club
Bashing us with their "beliefs"
Weary of never finding
Where the ends meet
Weary of naked hatred
In the streets

The scripture says
"Be not weary in well-doing
For in due season we shall reap
If we faint not"

Maybe that means
If you are tired of this mess,
Show some love
In your own neighborhood
Do good unto each other
Then maybe one day -- The meek shall inherit the earth.

I hate Christmas

I hate Christmas
Every winter it comes after me
Like the flu
I'm allergic to all the extra work
There is to do
Decorating, shopping, baking
Sending cards and preparing
To make merry
While drowning in debt
The desire to buy more
Just leaves me depressed

Everyone gets infected by the virus
Of consumerism
Except the poor
You see,
We punish ourselves for the inability
To lavish gifts on our loved ones
Feelings of inadequacy fill my shopping cart
As that is all I can afford
Wearily I languish
Among worn-out piles of stuff
We're afraid to get rid of
Because we know we can't afford more

So while my stuff fills my space
And my wallet is a disgrace
I can't bring myself to buy you a thing
That will sit around and add to your stuff
No, I can only give you things you can consume
Like wine or food

Or maybe a handmade gift from my heart
Like a hat or a scarf?
I know you think that's hokey
But low key
That's the best I can do

But wait, wait
This Grinch has had a break-through

This year I'm gonna give you something REALLY special for Christmas
I am going to spend my only asset on you

I'm gonna make TIME for you,

I am going to show up
I'm gonna hang out with you
I'm gonna make you laugh
I'm gonna make you happy
Even if it's only for a moment

I'm gonna make you feel loved
I'm gonna make you AWARE
Of how special you are to me
I'm gonna make your life better
As a result of being a friend to me
I'm gonna make your Christmas special
And bring all the love, joy and happiness of the season
Right to your door
The wrapping paper looks the same
As my face did before
But the bow I've applied
Is my prettiest smile
That reaches all the way to my heart
And it's just for you
'cause that's how seeing you
Makes me feel

So this year for Christmas
I'm gonna give you the gift that keeps on giving
I'm gonna spend time with you.
Because I love you
And we already have too much stuff.

Jesus loves the little children

"Jesus loves the little children
All the children of the world
Red and yellow, black and white
They are precious in His sight
Jesus loves the little children of the world"

I wish his followers did too
They don't
They just love birth and the idea of life
For too long the Religious White
    I mean Religious Right
Have tried to inflict their morality upon us
A lot of nice, white, church-going folks have been hoodwinked
In an effort to insulate believers from new people and new ideas
They are taught to fear others
And how they are just a bit better than those others

That is NOT what Jesus would do

Every religion has some version of the Golden Rule
"Do unto others as you would have them do unto you"
That means all others
But others really are the problem, aren't they?

Some group always has to be the other
Mexicans, Muslims, Asians, African-Americans, Jews
Rich people, poor people, LGBTQ people, disabled people,
Crips
Bloods
Vegans

Every new group of immigrants has their turn at being "other"
Just ask someone in a headscarf

And then ask yourself,
"Haven't we been brainwashed enough?"
When will we get tired of living in fear?
And debt? And squalor?
When will we realize we are more alike than different?
When will we band together and
REVOLT against the tyranny of the rich?
When will we demand Universal Healthcare?
When will we take care of our Veterans?
When will we protect our land and water?
When will we value our differences and learn from each other?
When will the richest nation in the world relieve its own poverty-
stricken?
When will we finally start coming together in the melting pot
To focus on the common good?
Forget all the lies you've been told
Friendship is worth more than gold.

Our only enemy is the one who would deny a hungry child food,
Or evict a woman from her home
Or refuse a man a sick-bed
Our enemy drops bombs on foreign children
Our enemy is US
Our government
In a shambles
Hijacked by big money interests
Flames fanned by barfly media
White men, I know it's hard,
But you have to let go of the notion of supremacy

It is literally killing us
Black lives matter
Female lives matter
Our lives matter
Let's make sure our lives matter, together
Red and yellow, brown, black and white,
We must band together so we can fight
ALL POWER TO THE PEOPLE

Divide

Divide and conquer
Divisions
Diversity
Don't be fooled by diversity
When what we need
Is inclusivity
Time for divisions has passed
No more separation
By gender, race or class

Because each one of us is human
Made in the image of God
But currently a pitiful reflection
Of God's magnificent creation

Assigning each level, a status
A value
A worth
Based on the exterior
Based on levels of privilege
And that my white brothers is
Where the trick is
Most of the people
With money and power
Are white men
So they told you
Only white men should have
Money and power

You thought that meant all white men
Just like they wanted you to
With that seed of division sown
Your disdain for "others" has grown
Somehow you didn't end up rich

But you could make sure you stayed at
The top of the pitch
By reducing the humanity of those beneath you
Worse yet,
Preserving that order as the way of the land
Breaking the commandment not to
Take the Lord's name in vain
And GD you have become
So vain and greedy
So selfish that you refuse to help the needy
Blaming them for the inferiority
You thrust upon them
In a self-defeating exercise in division
You poor thing
After all of your "eye for an eye"
You are blind and cannot see
That unity
Is the only way for humanity
To defeat the evil forces of greed
That keep us divided
For their needs
Keep us distracted
With intersectionality
While they steal all the feed
And keep us fighting over crumbs
Focused on the circus in front of us
Feeding the futility of brutal injustice

Because the powerful hold all the money
But they know they can only use it to control us
When we are divided
Because together
We the people
Can take back
Democracy
All we have to do

Is value every person as a human
Who should share in the bounty
Of our great country

The Lord said, "That which you do
To the least of these, you do unto me"
You would never treat Jesus so cruelly.
Did you forget he was an Ethiopian Jew?
You have never understood his teachings, have you?
Because the Christianity you've been served
Is a poison stew
Of hatred and misogyny
Taught to your progeny
With no questioning
To serve the status quo of the greedy
It is time for good people to rise up
And overturn the tables of the
Money changers in the house of the Lord

Feed the hungry, clothe the naked,
House the homeless and visit the hopeless
Do the things together that make your heart sing

Amalgamation
Amalgamation is the action, process or result of combining or uniting

I am a messy amalgamation
Of every experience I've ever had
Everywhere I've ever been
Everything I've ever seen
Of every song I've ever heard
Everyone I've ever met
Because we are all connected
You were a part of me
before I knew you

Knowing you are part of me
and I am part of you
allows me to love you
but more importantly,
allows me to love me
from the crown of my head
to the soles of my feet
I can embrace what society calls
My imperfections
As the markings of beauty
That they are

Because my hair is the color
Of golden honey
Splashed with sunshine
That could never fit
Inside a box
That is filled with chemicals
To control our brains
By holding beauty
Just out of reach

So I will never believe
I am good enough
The way I am

Time has stripped away
Streaks of my hair color
Leaving behind dramatic racing stripes
To remind me that
We are running out of time

My sparkly green eyes
Are wide open
And dotted with flecks of gold
To catch the light
Of love all around us

My magpie mouth
Spouts bursts of truth
That were swirling
All around you
Cobbled together from
Familiar phrases
But truth is hard to take
So it comes in phases
Sometimes in the words
Sometimes in the spaces

My skin is the color of spilt milk
Mixed with
Blood
And sweat
And tears
That's why I'm pink
Unless I've burned or broiled

All the way to vermillion

And I am never tan
Because I'm not supposed to be
That's not part of my beauty

See beauty shouldn't be
A judgement, achievement or measurement
A line you can cross
Like pass or fail
My beauty
Your beauty
Is in every gentle gesture
In every shared look
In every tiny spark of connection between us
That is where beauty grows
From kindness and love
Binding us
like atoms
One to another
And reminding us
We are all a part of this earth

But we have been drowning in this swamp
For far too long
Heads barely above the surface
Some, not able to survive
The evil mire
A vicious, viscous crude
Forming itself
From a bubbling ooze
Of greed and hatred
Gobbling up all the resources
It has grown enormous
Threatening to engulf us
We can only save ourselves
When we work together

Forming a human chain
Of brotherly love
To KUM
BAH
YAH
Each other out of the swamp
And drain it for good
For the good of We the People

It will evaporate
When we decide
That each person is worthy
That every human alive
Has a much value
As the unborn
Even if they are born brown
When we finally structure our society
To reflect what we SAY we believe
Then every person will be treated equally

AND WE CAN DO IT – TOGETHER
So join the amalgamation
That is me
And everyone like me
And everyone nothing like me
Only by rising up together
and VOTING, protesting, occupying and organizing
Can we finally be free.

Lightning Source UK Ltd.
Milton Keynes UK
UKHW020948060821
388423UK00013B/1077